Table of Contents

In Memory of

Bay Bea

Experiences
Along the Way

Joe Andrews

Experiences Along the Way

Library of Congress Cataloging-in-Publication Data

Andrews, Joe.
    Experiences along the way/Joe Andrews.
        p. cm.
    ISBN 1-57779-044-8
    1. Horse--Training. 2. Human-animal communication. I. Title.

SF287 .A63 2002
636.1'0835--dc21

                                                                    2002027747

The information contained in this book is complete and accurate to the best of our knowledge. All recommendations are made without guarantee on the part of the author or Alpine Publications, Inc. The author and publisher disclaim any liability with the use of this information.

For the sake of simplicity, the terms "he" or "she" are sometimes used to identify an animal or person. These are used in the generic sense only. No discrimination of any kind is intended toward either sex.

Editing: Dianne Nelson
Design: Laura Newport
Cover and Text Illustrations: Kim Andrews

First printing 2002

1 2 3 4 5 6 7 8 9 0

Printed in the United States of America.

Bay Bea

When Bay Bea first came to us she was a six-year-old brood mare, pregnant with her fourth foal. She was seriously under weight and her foal was due in two months. We were told she had been broke to ride when she was two, but she had not been ridden in several years. After her foal was weaned, we started to train Bay Bea as a riding horse. We found a lot of old baggage. Bay Bea was extremely cinchy, she was terrified of arenas, and she pulled back when she was tied. There was no indication that she had ever been ridden. It would have been easier to start a horse from scratch.

We treated Bay Bea with respect, asking instead of insisting and thanking her instead of demanding more. We communicated through pressure and release. We accepted any miscommunication as our own fault. We rewarded her for trying; we did not punish her for failing. We allowed her to exercise her flight instinct and were careful not to overconstrain her. We solved problems by looking at them from her perspective—not by looking for another piece of equipment.

Bay Bea rewarded us with her trust. She became light and responsive and would willingly do whatever we asked. She taught us about different gaits, and we learned that she could perform nine. Bay Bea was a special horse. I am thankful I had the opportunity to know her.

Joe Andrews

My Horse

His life is in my feeble hands,
the noble gallant steed;
his care is on my shoulders,
to meet his every need.

Taken from the open range
where he could live life free;
I've kept him from his family band
and asked for loyalty.

So what have I to offer,
to him in recompense,
for giving me his life
to live inside a fence?

To be a worthy leader
on whom he can rely;
to see the smallest change,
reward the slightest try.

With feel, timing, balance,
achieve true unity.
To make my partner's life worth more,
because he lives with me.

Foreword

The best way I can think of to describe the relationship that is possible between a horse and a person is to tell you about my favorite horse, Chip.

My neighbor asked me for help teaching her horse to pick up his feet. She had rescued him from abuse and he was virtually unmanageable. She had his feet trimmed when he was gelded. Having him anesthetized was the only way to do it; he would chase you out of his pen, biting and kicking, if you tried to get too close to him.

When I first saw Chip, I liked him. He was a stocky, old-style "bulldog" quarter horse with large eyes and a pronounced jaw. I saw lots of potential but he was scared to death. I knew it would take time to gain his confidence. I stayed with him until I was able to touch his shoulder and massage his neck under his thick, matted mane. He gave me a look that could only come from an abused animal, saying, "You are one in a million humans I could trust." That look moved me; I wished he were mine. Over the next few months I worked on gentling Chip and gaining his confidence. I got to the point where Chip would let me halter him, groom him, and pick up his front feet.

I moved and lost contact with my neighbor. Several months later she called, asking if I wanted Chip. She had not been able to train him herself and had sent him to a trainer. The trainer had halter-broke Chip, gotten on his back twice, and managed to trim his hind feet by squeezing Chip against the wall of his stall. My neighbor did not have the time to work with Chip, and the horse was becoming unmanageable again. If I would work with him, she would give Chip to me! Chip was in desperate need of having his feet trimmed; that was my first project. I worked with Chip slowly, patiently, and consistently—on his timetable, not mine. When he was ready, he stood for the farrier like an old pro. I spent several months doing ground work, developing Chip's trust, before getting in the saddle. I discovered things that really set him off, like the jingle of a chain, or the snap of a bug zapper. It saddened me to know these reactions had their roots in abuse. In working through these problems, Chip developed such trust and willingness that his eyes would look at me with almost eerie concentration, as if to look into my mind to see what I wanted next.

Chip has flourished in his new life and has rewarded me many times over for helping him. Chip takes care of my over-seventy mother-in-law on trail rides. Chip helps me give riding lessons to adults who have always wanted to learn to ride, and he is the greatest teacher for our young horses—he disciplines them when necessary, plays with them, and even shares his food with them. The potential I saw, and that special look, have become a dream come true.

Kim Andrews

Introduction

It Takes More Than Technique

I would like to pass on to you something that was handed down to me. It is a nontraditional approach to training horses. This approach develops a relationship with a horse based on trust, understanding, and communication. It comes from adjusting to fit the individual horse you are dealing with at any particular moment. The best way to describe this way of helping horses, without it sounding too much like a recipe, is to share my actual experiences with you. If it were possible, I would sit down with you on a grassy hillside in the warm afternoon sun some late spring day and swap stories about the horses we have ridden. Short of that, I offer you the stories in this book. Let me start by introducing myself.

The son of missionary parents, I spent my early years on the Duck Valley Indian Reservation in northern Nevada. It was ranching country, where most people raised registered Herefords and alfalfa hay. We lived in town, and most of my horse riding experiences consisted of riding Smoky, my grandfather's horse, when we visited his farm in southern Idaho.

I have a distinct memory of a severe fall I took at about nine years of age. This memory revisited me years later in the form of a vivid flashback. The pinto pony I was riding was trying his hardest to keep up with his friend, a larger palomino mare that was galloping down the side of the road. I remember the feeling of being totally out of control—and then the saddle slipped. I fell into the bar ditch and ended up against a fence post. I got a lump on my head and my ribs hurt something awful. The next day I had the nicest horseshoe-shaped bruise on my backside. After that, I don't think I rode a horse again except for a few rides on Smoky—until I met Kim.

Kim loved horses. While we were dating, she talked me into renting horses and riding with her. By the time we got married, Kim had me convinced that we would buy our own horses someday. We started saving spare change and using it to buy tack. One Christmas we bought each other saddles. I made a pair of saddle racks, and we kept our saddles in the corner of the bedroom. After we bought our first house, we were able to get our first horses and use the tack we had been collecting. It was on one of those first rides on our new horses that I had the flashback of my childhood fall. I saw the palomino mare. I smelled the freshly burned bar ditch. I was overwhelmed with the feeling of being totally out of control. I'm not sure which scared me the most—feeling the saddle start to slip or seeing and smelling things that weren't there.

Kim and I only wanted two horses. We had a camper and trailer and enjoyed taking our horses to the mountains on weekends. One Friday morning, just before a weekend trip, my mare Tippy presented us with a foal. It was a complete surprise, so we named him Sirprize and canceled our camping trip. When Sirprize had become my main riding horse, and his mother was hardly getting any use, we decided to sell the mare so that we could get back to having just two horses. Within a couple of months of selling Tippy, we were given Chip. Because we couldn't seem to only have two horses, we decided to try to get the horses to pay for themselves. Things just got out of hand from that point.

When I first became interested in training horses, I wasn't thinking of horsemanship—I was looking for answers to problems. I would go to clinics, thinking maybe this person would have the answer. My horse, however, didn't always respond the way the horse at the clinic responded. I began to understand that these clinicians had something I didn't have. As I became aware of horsemanship, I could see there was more to it than learning a certain technique. Different techniques were needed to fit different situations. I thought that horsemanship must be the ability to know which technique to use. With that in mind, I set out to develop a large tool kit of techniques gathered from different sources.

I went to see clinicians like Tom Dorrance, Ray Hunt, Buck Brannaman, John Lyons, and Pat Parrelli whenever they were in my area. I studied their books and videos, along with other books and tapes by classically trained authors. I applied these techniques to a variety of horses, in a variety of situations. As valuable as I found these techniques, what helped me understand horsemanship the most was a change in my attitude toward training. I found I needed to work with each horse as an individual, adjusting my actions to fit that horse. And, I was introduced to the idea of actually communicating my intention to the horse through the feel I present, rather than conditioning a horse to respond without thinking to a specific cue.

A mental connection occurs when you work with this kind of feel. I have seen horses change how they are acting simply because I took hold of the lead rope. It is like shaking hands with fifty different people. Some of those handshakes would feel good to you, some would be too firm, some would be too soft, and some would make you want to go wash your hands. If your job depended on how people felt about your handshake, you would learn how to have a handshake that felt good. Horsemanship runs deeper than learning a set of principles. It is about developing the skill to fit the individual horse—to offer that good handshake and make a mental connection.

It takes experience, measured not only in time but also in the variety of horses you work with, to develop this skill. I hope that the stories in this book will help you develop your own horsemanship skills. So, let me tell you a story or two. . . .

Socializing Prairie

When Curl, Prairie's mother, was getting close to the time she should deliver, we put her in a paddock at the front of the barn where she and her foal would have plenty of room and shelter. There was a gate between her paddock and the large paddock where the rest of our horses were kept. After Prairie was born, we witnessed an amazing interaction between horses at the gate.

For the first few days, neither mare nor foal went near the gate. If Prairie started to wander in that direction, Curl would hurry over and herd him back. During the next stage of this development, Curl and Prairie would go over to the gate, but Curl would keep the other horses away. She would squeal and kick anytime a horse got near. This went on for several weeks before Curl allowed the other horses near her foal. When we noticed Curl letting Prairie stay by the gate with the other horses while she went a short distance away, we decided it was time to open the gate and allow them into the herd for brief periods of time.

The next few weeks were quite interesting. It was as if Curl had a plan to socialize her foal so that he would not get hurt by the other horses. As we saw the stages of this plan unfold, we increased the time the gate was open until we no

2

longer needed to shut it. Curl started by allowing Prairie to wander around the big paddock as he pleased, but every time he got near another horse, she would rush over and chase that horse off. It didn't take long before the other horses worked at avoiding that little foal, which seemed to be what the mare was trying to accomplish at this stage.

Next, we noticed Curl letting Prairie get near the other horses—even jump on them or bite them—but she was there in all her fury if they tried to strike back. The next stage was fascinating. Curl started letting the other horses discipline her foal when he abused them, but she was right there if they carried it too far. I was amazed at the clarity of her line. If the discipline did not stop as soon as Prairie began to back off, Curl, the enforcer, was right there. When Curl was satisfied with how the other horses treated her foal, she spent more and more time away from Prairie and let him run with the others.

With Curl spending more time away from Prairie, and Prairie spending more time with the other horses, we began to take Curl out and work with her. Prairie never seemed too upset by his mother's absence. Over a couple of weeks, we increased the time that we had Curl out until we moved her to another pen for weaning. Kim and I marveled at how well the process worked when we let the horses tell us what they were ready for at each stage.

An Experiment in Communication

M arsha asked me to work with Fancy. Fancy had always been a spunky foal, but now that she was getting bigger, actions that were cute when she was small were becoming dangerous. I took my halter and lead rope and we walked into the weanling paddock together. Marsha kept the other weanling occupied while I worked with Fancy.

When I asked Fancy to follow a feel past me, she responded in the only way she knew how. In her mind, people were play toys—something to bite, kick, or leave. When she tried to bite, I used the tail of the lead rope to drive her shoulder away. When she tried to kick, I pulled her head around to move her hip over. I found myself having to firm up more than I thought this six-month-old filly should have to endure, just to protect myself. Things went on like this for a while without much improvement.

Trying to think of how to communicate in a way Fancy could understand, I decided to mimic the action of a horse. With both of us standing still, I turned my back to Fancy. I was in front of her, as if I were leading her on the end of the lead rope. From this position, with the intent of getting her to take a step back, I took a step back toward her. I paused briefly and waited for a response. Not receiving a response, I raised my foot in a deliberate fashion and put it down. Again

I paused and waited for a response. Still not getting a response, I took another step back and kicked. The flat sole of my boot made contact with Fancy's chest. My intention was just to get Fancy to take a step back. I felt if I communicated that to her, she would be more inclined to follow my direction on the lead rope. I was completely surprised by the scope of the change this created.

Fancy jumped back and seemed surprised. She stayed out at the end of the lead rope for a minute or so while I asked her to lead up with a light feel. I worked back and forth at an angle, releasing for each step. Soon she was standing next to me. I rubbed Fancy all over. She was calm, quiet, and respectful. She made no attempt to bite or kick. I directed Fancy out onto a circle and she responded very well. I yielded her hindquarters away, yielded her shoulder away, and drew her back to me with a very light feel in the lead rope. Fancy was right with me.

I'm not advocating that we kick our horses whenever they don't do what we want. The important thing is not that I kicked Fancy—it is that I got a response from her. If she had backed away when I backed toward her, that would have been enough. If I had stopped short of kicking her without getting a response, I would have reinforced her idea about people. By communicating with Fancy in a way she understood, I got a change in her feet that affected a change in her mind. That is the core of good horsemanship.

Charm's First Ride

M y goal in horse training is to develop the horse's ability to understand my intent through the feel I present. It is *not* to create a system of conditioned response cues. If a horse is not bothered by me, and what I am doing is not upsetting to the horse, the horse's natural curiosity and desire to please can make this a fun, rewarding, and relatively short process.

Kim and I have a six-month-old filly that we bought as a weanling. She is curious—not fearful, but respectful. Within two weeks after we bought her, Charm was doing ground work, working over obstacles, and leading with just a hand under the chin. It didn't seem like we did much to get this; mostly we blended in with her, directing a little and encouraging her to use her curiosity. Our actions were guided by the attitude, "What can I do to best help her understand my intentions?"

Even at this young age we are preparing Charm for work she will be expected to do later in life. We simulate the feel of a saddle by leaning over her, wrapping our arms around her and squeezing a little. We yield her hindquarters away with pressure from our hands on her side where our legs will be when we ride her. We yield her shoulders away by placing our hands on her neck where the rein will eventually be. With a picture in mind of what we want Charm to do, we are quick to adjust and blend in if we see something different shaping up. Although we accomplish a lot of "training," this training occurs primarily through our interactions while we take care of her.

One day, when Kim and I went in to clean the pen, Charm just had to be right in the middle of things. Rather than chase her off, Kim took her for a little ride. Placing her arms on Charm's sides, Kim guided Charm around the pen in little circles and figure-eights as if she were steering a riding horse with her legs.

When Charm's curiosity drew her back to me and the manure scooping, Kim blended in, placing her arms as if she had asked for Charm to turn that way. Then Kim would keep Charm's momentum going and guide her away from me again. By the time I finished cleaning the pen, Kim had Charm guiding lightly off of "leg pressure" and Charm had had her first "ride."

Getting Started
With Prairie

W hen I approached the gate, Prairie was lying down just
inside the barn. I thought the commotion of the
wheelbarrow would disturb him, but he didn't bother to get
up. He was still lying there when I finished cleaning the pen,
so I decided to give him some attention. I walked around to
where he could see me coming and approached him. Prairie
raised his head but didn't get up. I petted him until he let out
a sigh and put his head down again. I was pleased he was
that comfortable with me. Other foals we had raised went
through a phase at Prairie's age where we couldn't catch them
for a few weeks.

When Prairie was born, Kim and I decided to minimize
the amount we handled him. The first day we didn't touch
him at all. We caught him one time on the second day for the
vet. We never forced ourselves on him again; we waited for
him to approach us on his terms. Before Prairie was two
weeks old, we noticed something remarkable.

Sometimes Prairie seemed to think of us as old friends,
and other times he acted like we were dangerous predators.
This behavior was not random but was tied closely to how
his mother felt about our presence. There was a strong emo-
tional tie between Prairie and the mare. If our approach

made her suspicious, Prairie would not come near us. We found it necessary to stay mentally relaxed and not be on a mission when we entered their space. It was also important to take time to say hello to Mom and get her relaxed with us before focusing on the foal. As we presented ourselves this way, Prairie gained confidence and we were able to interact with him more.

Going about our daily routine, Kim and I paid attention to Prairie whenever he looked us up. We let him go when he left, figuring he'd had as much of us as he could handle at that time. We were careful not to encourage behavior that seemed cute now but would be dangerous when he got bigger. Expecting Prairie to be well mannered and polite, we rewarded him when he was and redirected him when he wasn't. We did have specific things in mind for him to do, but we didn't have an agenda to teach them to him. Watching for opportunities, we encouraged those actions when they were about to happen.

When we saw him about to step his hindquarters over, we put a hand on his side and asked for that step. If he got in a tight spot, we helped him back out with our hand on his chest. We tried to never miss an opportunity to back up and draw him to us when he was interested in our being there. It was amazing how quickly Prairie learned when we directed him a little and let him use his natural curiosity to find the answer.

Keeping a clear picture in our mind of the perfectly polite adult horse, we guided Prairie toward that ideal. Soon Prairie became a confident, friendly gentleman who could not get enough attention.

Picking Up Princess

We are not always presented with ideal situations. Sometimes we have to do a lot of adjusting and be willing to take the time to keep horse and human safe. Kim and I had been musing about this for weeks. Our friends were purchasing a weanling filly for their son's birthday. Kim had been giving Paul lessons for about a year. In preparation for getting his own filly, he had been working with our young horses. Now it was time for us to pick up Princess.

We had suggested that Princess be weaned with other foals in a corral and be given about two weeks away from her mother before she was moved to her new home. That would give them some time to begin to interact with her and reduce her stress by making this change in her life gradually. As circumstances would have it, things were not done that way. When the mare's owner decided it was time to wean Princess, the filly was run into a small pen by herself and our friends were told to come get their horse. We made arrangements to pick up Princess that evening at 7:00; we didn't have an opportunity to work with her before then. What a daunting task it was, to teach this baby to accept human touch, to become comfortable with a lead rope, to allow us to put a halter on her head, to give to pressure, to lead, to load into a trailer, and to travel safely—starting so late at night! Our first priority was that Princess was not to get hurt, and we were not to get hurt. Safety was everything—time was not an issue.

I had a previous commitment that evening, so Kim went to meet Mike and his wife at the farm where Princess was waiting. There was junk all over the place—treasures to some. Kim negotiated the narrow, curved drive between a large manure pile and the round pen to a small turnaround. Access to the long row of pens was blocked by a hot walker; therefore, backing up to Princess's pen was not an option. Kim found herself in a challenging situation. Not having had much human contact and having just lost the security of her mother, Princess was flighty. Princess's pen, near the far end of the alley, was in poor repair. Jagged, broken boards, exposed nails, and piles of the kind of junk that collect on a farm over the years severely limited the amount of pressure that could be safely put on her. The foal next to Princess had a ghastly gash on the back of its front leg from an exposed T-post.

When Mike and Kim entered Princess's pen, they found one thing in their favor: Princess, who was hungry, had just been given a few flakes of hay. Her strong desire to get something to eat momentarily overrode her fear of people; therefore, touching her was not a problem. The hay drew her back when she left. As Kim started to introduce the halter, Princess, less hungry now, didn't want anything to do with it and moved off. Determined to take the time it took to get this done without injury, Mike stationed himself about halfway down the pen, and Kim stayed near the hay by the gate, creating a kind of human round pen. Each time Princess ran past them they would reached out to touch her. As she quieted down, Mike and Kim gradually worked their way closer and closer together.

Princess was making them devise ways to encourage her to want to be with them. Kim began to put a little more pressure on Princess by tossing a lead rope over Princess's back when the filly came near. Mike tried to make things soft and comfortable when Princess came near him. To get Princess even more comfortable with Mike, he switched places with Kim and let Princess have some more hay, because by then she was hungry again. While Princess was eating, Mike approached and retreated with the halter. Princess moved away a little, but for the most part, Mike could touch Princess's ears, head, and neck. Princess would not allow the halter to go over her nose, but Mike slipped the lead rope around her neck and took it off and put it on again several times.

Kim knew from experience what could happen the first time a young, nervous horse was asked to give to the pressure of the lead rope. She had to get Princess out of that pen. There was no room to drift with her, and the fences were so dangerous Princess would likely get hurt if she slammed into them, or she might flip over in a state of panic. By this time it was 9:30 p.m. Again, time really wasn't an issue, but it was interesting keeping track of how long each step in the progression took.

Mike and Kim discussed their plan to get Princess from the pen to the trailer. Mike's wife was stationed at the gate. After she opened the gate, she was to stand in the alley, blocking the path to the other horses. Kim would run to the other end of the alley, by the hot walker, and block the stallion pens. Because Mike could only get a lead rope around Princess's neck, Kim talked to him about keeping a forty-five-degree angle on Princess. That forty-five-degree angle was his safety and power position to disengage the hind end. Kim mentioned all the things Princess might do out of self-preservation before she started to look for the release. And the most important thing was for Mike to NOT LET GO.

When Mike's wife opened the gate, Princess shot out with Mike in tow. Princess, weighing about 300 pounds, dragged Mike, weighing about 185 pounds, toward the mares before she turned. Mike kept the forty-five-degree angle the entire way and never let go. Princess ran again, Mike still in tow. This time, when she turned, she ran in circles around Mike

By approaching and retreating, Mike asked Princess to stand near the trailer. She quickly became comfortable standing at the back of the trailer and sniffing it but would go no further.

It was after 11:00 p.m. when I arrived. Mike and Kim were tired and were running out of ideas. I had another lead rope with me so that Princess could be haltered properly. By this time, she willingly accepted the halter. Mike had been reassuring Princess all evening by rubbing and petting her. Princess had become comfortable with his touch, and she was comfortable with me. I began asking her to step from side to side, trying to encourage her to try a step into the trailer. It looked, for a moment, like we might be making progress. Princess brought her hind feet under her for balance and lifted her front leg up to paw the trailer. Our hope, however, was short-lived. That was the extent of Princess's try, and it seemed to convince her that we were asking her to do an impossible task.

Princess had hit a plateau. She was comfortable with us, and she was comfortable standing just outside the trailer. It was time to make outside the trailer uncomfortable and inside the trailer a good place. Kim stood to the side of Princess and tapped her croup, stopping with the slightest indication that Princess was thinking about going forward. I was inside the trailer, encouraging Princess with the lead rope. Kim and I became good at timing our releases equally. It was as if we were reading each other's mind. Princess began to understand. She tried many times to lift herself into the trailer. Knowing her final try would be a big one, I moved to the front of the trailer to give Princess plenty of room. She took all the room I gave her with one big leap into the trailer. It didn't take Princess long to find the hay we had for her. Petting her as she ate, I made sure she was content before I slipped the halter off, leaving her loose in the trailer.

It was 1:00 a.m. when we made the short drive to Princess's new home. She was still eating the hay when we pulled in. I stepped into the trailer and haltered Princess like she had been doing it her entire life. She softly leapt out of the trailer and was led to her new paddock without incident. We had accomplished our goal—Princess had not been hurt, and we had not been hurt. It was incredible how much Princess learned in a few hours. We were all impressed with how her understanding developed with each step. Princess was a good find. Paul is one lucky kid. We knew he would be happy when he woke up.

Soaking Whinnie's Foot

C arol called me to see if I would be able to help her. Her horse, Whinnie, had an abscess in her hoof, and the vet said they needed to soak the hoof for ten minutes every day. Carol was beside herself with frustration because she could not get Whinnie to keep her foot in the bucket for one minute—let alone ten.

Whinnie was a two-year-old Thoroughbred filly, full of youthful enthusiasm that sometimes displayed itself quite dramatically. Carol's husband had cut the top off a five-gallon plastic pail, leaving the sides about six inches high. They had tried to put Whinnie's foot into the bucket, but she kept pulling her foot back, spilling the betadyne solution. Further attempts were getting Whinnie upset, and she was having trouble keeping her front feet on the ground.

I started by asking Whinnie to lower her head. Presenting a light feel with one hand on the lead rope and my other hand over her poll, I released as soon as Whinnie's head started to go down. When Whinnie seemed to follow the feel of my hands without resistance, I gave her a break and petted her. Next, I asked her to step a front foot back. I looked to see which foot was in a position to go back and tipped her nose over that foot. With slight pressure from the lead rope, I

asked for that foot to move back. As soon as the foot started
to move, I released. Working this way, I progressed until
Whinnie would step either foot back or forward without
resistance.

I had Carol put the betadyne solution in another bucket.
I picked up Whinnie's foot and washed the dirt off it. Placing
the plastic pail over her hoof, I set them down together. I
stood there watching how Whinnie was balanced. If she started to shift her weight off that foot, I asked her to shift it back.
If she was going forward, I would set her back. If she was
going backward, I would set her forward. Using the same feel
I had used to step her feet, I was able to keep her foot from
taking a step. When I had established that I could keep
Whinnie's foot in place, Carol poured the betadyne solution
into the bucket.

We stood there for the required ten minutes without incident. I picked up Whinnie's foot and dried it off. Carol had
some dressing and a duct tape bandage her husband had pre-
made. Unfortunately, the bandage folded prematurely, stick-
ing to itself, and Carol was unable to get it apart. In order to
keep Whinnie's foot clean while Carol made up another
bandage, we emptied the pail and I put Whinnie's foot back
in it. Whinnie and I stood there for another five minutes or
so with her foot in the bucket. When the new bandage was
ready, we packed and bandaged the foot.

7

Catching Blackie

J oyce had gotten in over her head. She had no idea how to
deal with what was going on with her horse, and she needed help. When I asked what the problem was, she said her
horse had broken three lead ropes and two halters. Blackie
was a two-year-old Joyce had bought, along with another
young horse, about three months ago. Neither horse had
been haltered previously, and the person who sold Joyce the
horses had told her to keep the halters on until the horses
were gentled enough to catch and halter easily. Joyce had
been making great progress with Blackie's training until the
another horse died when he got hung by his halter in the
pasture. After that incident, Joyce decided she should not
leave the halter on all the time; however, when she took the
halter off Blackie, he "just got wild."

When I arrived at Joyce's farm, I wasn't thrilled with the
situation. Blackie was in a rectangular, mesh-wire, T-post pen
with an older horse. The pen was an appropriate size, but the
fencing was too low and flimsy to allow me to work safely
with a wild horse. I knew I would not be able to put much
pressure on Blackie, but I could tell she was going to be pushy.
As I entered the pen, Blackie ran into the older horse like he
wasn't even there and viciously bit him for not moving. When

Blackie came around again, she kicked at my head as she passed me. It was a well-aimed, well-timed kick that would have connected if we hadn't been twelve feet apart. I stayed in the middle of the pen and did nothing more than keep track of where Blackie was until she settled down enough to quit running. Having the older horse in the pen gave me the opportunity to show Blackie that I intended no harm. I walked up to the older horse and rubbed him with my hand. Then I walked toward Blackie. When Blackie moved away, I walked toward her, careful not to put too much pressure on her. When Blackie stopped and looked at me, I walked over to the other horse and rubbed him again. As time progressed, Blackie let me get closer to her. Then she started to follow me a little when I walked away from her to pet the other horse. At that point, I took a little break. Stopping at a point where Blackie had followed me a few steps, I stood still. As long as Blackie's attention was on me, I did nothing. Whenever her attention started to wander, I would move a little—just enough to get her attention back.

Standing there gave me the opportunity to talk more to Joyce about the change that had happened in Blackie. She described how Blackie had stood at the spot in the field where the other horse had died for more than twenty-four hours without eating or drinking. We talked about what a traumatic experience it had been for Blackie. First, Blackie and her friend had been haltered for the first time in their lives. Then they had been taken away from the farm where they grew up. The final blow was having her friend hung by the halter. No wonder Blackie got wild; in her mind, she was fighting for her life.

Now that Blackie would stay facing me, I began approaching her a little at a time. I would move toward her a few steps, then back off a step or two. If she got ready to leave, I would move away. By moving in an arc—away from her head, but toward her hind end—I could get her to face up again. When I was able to get close enough, I held out my hand, let Blackie smell it, and walked away. As I repeated this approach-and-retreat scenario, the amount of time it took to get close to Blackie decreased, while the amount of time I could stay close to her increased. When Blackie seemed comfortable enough with me, I reached up and brushed her with my hand just before walking away. Soon Blackie was letting me stand beside her and rub her all over with my hand. I took the curry comb out of my pocket and began grooming her. She seemed relieved that she could trust me.

As I prepared to approach Blackie again, I organized the halter I had been holding over my arm. I walked up to Blackie, petted her neck with my hand, and then petted her with the halter. When she was comfortable with the halter rubbing her neck and face, I slipped it on and off her head. I wanted to catch and halter Blackie as many times as I could. I would walk up to her, put the halter on, do a little something, take the halter off, and walk away. At first, I just asked for Blackie to lower her head. Then I started bending her and moving her feet. It wasn't long before I could position Blackie wherever I wanted. She was understanding the feel through the lead rope and was confident that she was not in danger.

Joyce asked me if I could show her daughter how to do what I was doing with Blackie, because she was the one who would be working with the horse. I took the halter off Blackie and invited Wendy to come into the pen. Taking the halter, Wendy walked up to Blackie, petted her and put on the halter. I explained to Wendy how to communicate what she wanted Blackie to do by changing how the halter felt on Blackie's face, emphasizing that the lead rope was not there for pulling the horse around by her head. Wendy had a wonderful, natural feel about her. It was obvious that she and Blackie made a connection. Seeing the two of them working together exceeded every expectation I had about the change a horse could make in one session.

8

A Walk Around
The Buttes

P rince didn't get upset when the edge of the bank gave way under his feet. He backpedaled slowly with his hind feet, keeping his balance as he slid down with the loose dirt into the arroyo. I petted him as he stood there next to me with his head low, licking his lips. I was ahead of the riders at this point, working my way through the last of a series of arroyos. I knew it would be a while before we would meet up again, but I was anxious to tell them how well Prince was doing.

When Kim and I decided to ride with some friends at the Pawnee Buttes, I waffled about which horse to take. I wanted to use the opportunity to give one of our youngsters some experience but I didn't think any of them were ready for riding in country that rough. I decided to take Prince. He wasn't ready to ride, but it would be good to expose him to the terrain.

I saddled Prince and did some ground work while everyone else was getting ready. The control I had of Prince through the halter would be needed when the going got rough. The first arroyo still held some snow and ice due to its northern exposure. The riders elected to avoid these potentially slick areas by making a larger circle to the north. By cutting across, I could meet up with the group on the east side of the buttes.

Just before getting to the bottom of the arroyo, I had to coax Prince down a three-foot dropoff. He made a big jump and tried to rush off. I was glad I had developed the ability to control his feet through the lead rope. I cornered Prince and put him back where I wanted him. The trail up the other side was steep and narrow. Prince was a little bothered by the confinement and crowded me. I backed him off by sending a little life down the lead rope. Each time Prince needed extra support from me I offered a light suggestion but would do what it took to get the response I needed. When Prince came through, I would pause briefly and pet him.

The buttes were blocking the wind now that I was north of them. The warmth of the sun gave me the idea to let Prince pack my coat. I watched for the riders and angled my way across the flat prairie to meet them.

The labyrinth of arroyos fanning out east of the buttes presented a formidable challenge. After a brief reconnoiter, the riders decided to go further east where the arroyos were not as deep and the banks not as steep. I elected to cut across, leaving the bright, dry, vast plains for the damp shadows of the narrow canyons.

The maze I found myself in was not designed for human travel—it was made by water following the path of least resistance. The sandstone walls towered above me, offering only an occasional way out. It was with a certain level of excitement that I worked my way through the intricate pattern, looking for passages I could negotiate that would take me in the direction I needed to go.

I enjoyed seeing Prince's capabilities. He was really getting his hind end under him and staying balanced going down steep banks. He followed me willingly up anything I was able to climb. Because I had been consistent with Prince, I was not having to think much about where he was anymore. If the trail was wide enough, he walked beside me. When the trail narrowed, he fell in behind me, staying back about six feet. I felt like I was on a walk with my best friend—not training a young horse.

The Power of Intent

I find myself having to adjust to fit a variety of circumstances as I travel to different places. Sometimes it can be a little frustrating, but these situations often turn out to be great learning experiences. One of these frustrating experiences ended up being a great example about the power of intent.

I was looking forward to working with Badger. He had made a nice change in our last session. Working in the round pen, he had begun calming down and started to get hooked on. It was a warm, sunny day—the kind that makes me glad I work outside—and my mind was filling with lots of ideas about how I could build on our last lesson. When I arrived at the boarding stable, where I would be working with Badger, I noticed that the round pen was occupied by a couple of horses, a large hay feeder, and a water tank. I would have to work in the large arena behind the barn. I wouldn't be able to work with Badger loose, like I had planned to do in the round pen, but I could get a lot done on the halter and lead rope.

As I started to work, Badger was reluctant to lead past me on a circle. He seemed to be more concerned with the wheelbarrow-size manure piles that dotted the arena—evidence that the pens between the barn and the arena had been cleaned—than with understanding my intent. I tried to make my intent more clear, and that's when Sadie showed up. Sadie is a black-and-white Border Collie mix with a strong herding instinct. She began running back and forth behind Badger, nipping at his heels. At first I tried to ignore Sadie and focus on Badger. It was soon obvious that was not going to work. Next, I tried to discourage Sadie with the end of the lead rope. That turned out worse. It was not only ineffective on Sadie, it bothered Badger. I picked up my flag and waved it at the dog. Sadie's herding instinct was so strong, nothing I did discouraged her. By now Badger was leaning back on the lead rope, trying to escape the situation. I decided it was time to do something else.

I stopped Badger and began petting him to calm him down. I asked him to lower his head in order to reestablish some communication. When he lowered his head softly, in response to my feel, I asked him to flex laterally without moving his feet. Now that my intent was to not move Badger's feet, Sadie lost interest in us. She occupied herself by rolling in one of the manure piles nearby and preparing herself for a nap. I spent several minutes working peacefully with Badger, getting him softer in the halter, flexing laterally and vertically.

With Badger following my feel to bend so well, and Sadie off chasing rabbits in her dreams, I decided to try moving Badger out on a circle again. As soon as my intention changed—to move Badger's feet—Sadie sprang to life and began nipping at Badger's heels again.

10

Taming Blaze

While I may not be an expert on young stallion behavior, I do have some experience, having raised three of my own and having trained several for a breeding farm near me. I don't do anything different just because the horse is a stud. I've heard Ray Hunt say you need to ride a stallion as if he was a gelding. What I would say is, you should handle every horse the way you need to handle a stallion. Stallions are less tolerant of sloppy handling than mares and geldings. It is important to really have them with you mentally. You must be precise without being picky, and you must be just.

Blaze was a yearling stud colt when Kay called me. He had bitten or kicked everyone on her place. The last straw came when he smashed her against a fence. You could walk up and halter Blaze, but if you put any pressure on him, he would rear up and strike out. Kay did not have a round pen; all my work had to be done with a halter and lead rope in the thirty-five-acre pasture where Blaze lived with four older geldings. I worked with Blaze two days a week, using the same ground work I use with every horse. He got to the point where, after a ten minute warm-up, I could take off the halter and continue doing the same exercises at liberty, still in the thirty-five-acre pasture.

While I do have specific tasks I teach a horse, I hesitate to list them; that would sound too much like a recipe. As long as the tasks involve yielding, drawing, and developing communication through feel, you should be fine. Attitude is more important than the actual task. You need to do everything you can to help the horse understand what you are asking, as opposed to expecting the horse to do what you want just because you followed the instructions. Have a specific way in mind for the horse to move its feet, and develop the horse's ability to understand your intention through the feel that you present.

When I am working with a horse, I start with a plan in mind but adjust it to fit what that horse needs at that time. I may adjust my presentation, or I may use a different exercise. The fact that I did all my work with Blaze in a pasture with the halter and lead rope is an example of adjusting to fit the situation. Normally I would start working with a horse like this in a round pen.

Everything I did with Blaze, I treated as an exercise in understanding my intention. I would walk out into the pasture, carrying the halter over my arm. If Blaze moved away from me, I followed. If Blaze stopped and looked at me or came in my direction, I stopped and backed up—even if he was a long way off. When I got close to Blaze, I tried to make sure that the last move before we made contact was him coming toward me. After haltering Blaze, I led him to a flat area to work, away from the other horses. By the time Blaze was leading up real free, and I could place his feet anywhere I wanted them, he was with me enough to allow us to work without the halter. Initially, Blaze had some ye-haw moments, but we quickly developed a rapport. He actually seemed to like having some direction and an understanding of how he was supposed to behave. It felt good to him, and it felt good to me.

Building a Foundation

I am constantly amazed at what people consider "broke" riding horses. More often than I care to admit, I am asked to help people who are having a problem with their horse, only to hear a familiar story. When they bought their horse, they purchased it as a "broke" riding horse. After being scared or hurt, they realize they need help. When I start working with the horse, I find it is missing such important parts of its foundation, I can't believe anyone has ridden it, let alone represented it as a "broke" horse.

Sioux is a prime example. I first saw Bonnie riding Sioux on an Open Space trail. I had arrived about an hour early for an appointment and decided to walk the three-mile trail that encompassed the boarding facility. About halfway around the loop, I saw a flashy brown-and-white horse doing a stepping pace. Recognizing the soft gait, I asked the rider what kind of horse she had. Bonnie introduced me to Sioux, a spotted Missouri Fox Trotting Horse, and I told her I had Fox Trotters, too. Our conversation led to the fact that I helped people with their horses, and Bonnie asked me to leave one of my cards at the barn. She had been thinking she might need some lessons because she couldn't seem to get Sioux to settle down.

Several weeks later, at a demonstration Kim and I put on for the Larimer County Horseman's Association, Bonnie reintroduced herself to me. She said she definitely wanted to schedule some lessons. After we met on the trail, Bonnie's leg got squished going through a gate, and her knee swelled up. When she told her massage therapist what happened, the therapist recommended giving me a call. Back at the barn, Bonnie saw a flyer for the LCHA demonstration. Without realizing I was the one putting on the demonstration, she decided "Developing Manners Through Ground Work" was something she really needed. When she arrived at the demonstration and recognized me, Bonnie couldn't believe it. She had run into me too many times for her to ignore the situation any longer and decided she needed to work with me.

I was amazed that Bonnie had been riding Sioux. Sioux was such a nervous little mare, she couldn't even stand still and let me brush her. When I asked her to move over by touching her side, it was like pushing on a tree trunk. Cleaning between her teats was a project; Sioux kicked and squirmed away. Knowing that Bonnie had been riding her, I didn't expect saddling to be a problem, but Sioux pulled back hard against the lead rope when I tried to put my saddle pad on her back. Untying her, I saddled Sioux and headed for the round pen.

I didn't expect Sioux to know the ground work I use, but I was surprised at the stiffness and resistance she displayed. She acted like bending was a dangerous thing to do. Once I was able to move Sioux around and position her where I wanted, I climbed up on the fence and tried to bring her alongside me. Sioux was so afraid of me being above her that she wouldn't get anywhere near the fence. Attempts to encourage her to come in my direction resulted in her pulling back. When I did finally get in the saddle, Sioux acted like she had never supported a rider; she just wanted to go fast. I could not bend her or shape her body, and I had to ride with much more contact than I normally do. Slacking the reins was like opening the floodgates of a dam.

I decided that Sioux needed work much lower down the ladder. I tried to let her get comfortable with me by turning her loose in the arena and just waiting for her to look me up. I spent time grooming her, loose in the round pen. I massaged her and made sure there was no place she would not let me touch. I quietly moved her around with my hands, positioning her head and feet where I wanted them. I wanted to make being around me something that filled Sioux with understanding and calmness. I also wanted her to start looking for the intention in the feel I offered, confident that she would find a release.

I think we still have a ways to go with Sioux, but Bonnie is already having some better rides on her.

Saddling Abule

M y back ached, and my arms felt like they were six inches longer than they were three days earlier. My shoulders were sore from the cinch I had rigged up to help hold
the saddle. I was tired, but the feeling I got from seeing Abule
remain calm when I swung the saddle onto his back made it
all worth it.

Abule was a beautiful three-year-old bay Arab gelding I
was starting under saddle. He had responded well to all the
ground work preparation, but when it came to putting the
saddle on his back, it just wasn't going to happen. I decided
to back off on what I was asking of him and try to work up
to it in increments.

Using a small child's saddle that I could easily lift with one
hand, I rubbed him all over. Then I placed the small saddle on
his back and took it off. Over the next several days, I literally
put that saddle on and off his back a thousand times. I would
work on one side until that arm got tired, then switch sides.
After switching sides a couple of times, I would call it good for
that day.

When Abule got so comfortable with the child's saddle
that his expression didn't change when I was putting it on
him, I upgraded to a small adult synthetic saddle. I repeated
the same process with the larger saddle. First I rubbed him all

over with it, then put it on and off until my arm got tired and I switched sides. In a couple of days, Abule got just as comfortable with the synthetic saddle as he had with the smaller one.

At this point, I went back to my big saddle. While I could get it on him, he obviously was uncomfortable with it. Normally, I would expect that to get better rather quickly, but Abule seemed to be getting worse, not better. I decided to see if the problem was physical.

The chiropractor who examined Abule said there was no physical problem. He also said that Abule's reaction to the big saddle was normal for an Arab. In fact, he couldn't put his heavy roping saddle on either his wife's or daughter's horse. They both used lightweight synthetic saddles because they rode Arabs. I wasn't buying that, so I continued to work on getting Abule comfortable with my big saddle, even though progress was slow.

Several days later, I was grooming Abule at the hitch rail. Kim was using the round pen for a lesson. Abule had gotten a little more comfortable, so I thought I could saddle him in the open. I looped the lead rope around the hitch rail a couple of times and went to get my saddle. It was my intention to take Abule away from the hitch rail to saddle him, so that we would have plenty of room. As I approached Abule, I saw him get uncomfortable. I stopped about fifteen feet away and set my saddle down on the porch. Abule pulled away from the hitch rail and headed for the back fence. I realized then that it wasn't the saddle going on his back that bothered Abule—he was afraid of the saddle itself.

I decided to carry the saddle around with me whenever I was working with Abule. I thought if I just made it a part of his life, he would learn to accept it. Over the next three days, I carried that saddle between six and nine hours.

The first day I sat on a stump in the middle of Abule's pen with the saddle on my lap. Abule ran around the pen for half an hour before he stopped and came over to investigate it. When I reached up to pet him, he took off running again. It took another twenty minutes before Abule would stand there and let me pet him. When I stood up, holding the saddle at my side, Abule took off running again. It took another twenty minutes before he stopped to look at me. Within half an hour, he came over to investigate. I reached out to pet him, and that sent him running again. Finally, he allowed me to stand there and pet him. I hung out with him for a while, still holding the saddle, then left him for the day.

The next day I took the saddle with me into Abule's pen and stood in the center. He ran around for a few minutes then came over to check out the saddle. When I reached out to pet him, he went off again but not for long. When he came back, he stood there and let me pet him. At that point, I put a halter on him and took him out of the pen. Holding the lead rope and the saddle in one hand I groomed him with the other hand. The weight of the saddle caused me to change hands frequently, and that would make Abule scurry away. Keeping Abule bent, I let him move around me in a circle and drifted with him until I could continue grooming. He

would stop when I started rubbing him with the brush. By the time I had Abule groomed on both sides, he was less bothered by the saddle shifting when I changed hands.

On the third day, I haltered Abule and led him out of the pen with him doing nothing more than giving the saddle a sideways glance. I sent him around me in a circle by directing him out with my free hand. I bent him and disengaged his hind end by lifting the lead rope and stepping toward his flank. When Abule's feet stopped, I directed him back with the lead rope and then brought his shoulders across. I had to switch arms more frequently now that my muscles were so tired. After a while, Abule began to act as if I wasn't carrying the saddle anymore. He would stop calmly and stand quietly while I petted him. Finally!

I have never seen another horse that had such a problem with the saddle. I have never had to work so hard to get a horse to accept the saddle. I have never had the same feeling seeing a horse stand calmly for saddling. It was as if Abule decided that if I was willing to pack that big heavy thing around, he could, too.

13

Beauty

"Where's the camera?" Karen asked excitedly. She hurried toward the house, anxious to record what was happening. "No one is going to believe this if we don't get a picture!"

Bob and Karen had been sitting in the shade of their gooseneck trailer with Beauty's owner. When Karen saw me take my saddle off the fence, she came over to the round pen for a closer look. When Bob saw the saddle slide onto Beauty's back, and Beauty just stood there, he joined Karen. There was one minor glitch when I clumsily dropped the rear cinch. The buckle hit Beauty in the flank and she squirted forward, dropping my saddle on the ground. I calmed Beauty and set my saddle on her back again. This time I managed to cinch it up without startling her. That's when Karen went for her camera.

With Karen shooting pictures, I moved Beauty around on the end of the lead rope. Soon I was climbing the fence to give Beauty the experience of seeing someone above her. It didn't take long at all for Beauty to find a place to stand next to me. She really seemed to take comfort in being near me. I rubbed her, patted the saddle, leaned over so she could see me on both sides of her at the same time, and moved the off-side stirrup around. That's when Michael, Beauty's owner, left the shade and came down to the pen.

Putting my leg over Beauty's back several times, and rubbing my foot across her rump just behind the saddle, I satisfied myself that those things didn't trouble her. Staying committed to the fence, I briefly eased into the saddle. Having repeated that several times, to make sure it was not a fluke that Beauty stayed calm, I let go of the fence with one hand and petted Beauty's neck as I sat there on her back. It seemed like a good spot to stop for the day.

"I thought Beauty was supposed to be a dangerous horse," I heard Karen say as I was taking the saddle off and brushing Beauty's back.

"She is a dangerous horse," I joked. "Someone's going to get around her and start liking Arabs."

The first time I worked with Beauty, I had expected to spend the entire session in the pasture following her around, looking for an opportunity to back off and draw her to me. She had the reputation of being impossible to catch. As I approached, there were several other horses around her. I took my time, petting each one as I worked my way toward Beauty. By the time I got to her, Beauty was interested in getting some of that attention, too. I rubbed her a little, rubbed another horse that was within reach, rubbed Beauty again, and simply put a halter on her.

I led Beauty to the round pen, turned her loose, and began grooming her. If she stood still, I curried and brushed her. If she walked off, I drove her away—just a little faster than she left on her own. I would keep a little pressure on Beauty by walking toward her until she looked my way. By backing off, I encouraged her to stop with her attention on me. Then I would approach her and continue grooming. Soon Beauty was staying with me and was even following me around the pen. I had to drive her off so that I could work on catching her.

Alternating between working at liberty and doing ground work in the halter, I "caught" Beauty at least half a dozen times. I would walk right up to her, put my arm over her neck, and hold the nose band of the halter open. Beauty would look for the halter, put her nose in the opening, and slide it up her face. So much for being impossible to catch.

The next week, when I went back to work with Beauty, her owner asked if I could get her into a trailer. I only had an hour, and I needed to spend some time developing my ability to place her feet. I spent the first half-hour in the round pen getting Beauty's attention and moving her feet with the feel I had through the lead rope. When I could lead her past me, step her hip over, back her up, and step her shoulder over, I went to the trailer. With only half an hour left to work on trailer loading, I could not promise that Beauty would get in the trailer that day, but it would be a good start.

Beauty was apprehensive about the trailer. She stopped just before stepping on the ramp and was looking for a way to leave. I petted her and stepped her feet back and forth, just like I had done in the round pen. Soon Beauty's front foot stepped on the ramp. I praised her and petted her, then took her away from the trailer. I wanted to create a spot a little ways away from the trailer where Beauty could relax and be with me. I alternated between moving Beauty up to the trailer and taking her back to our nice place. When I sent Beauty away from our spot, I did as little directing as possible—just enough to keep her headed toward the trailer. When she stopped in front of the trailer, I directed her forward and encouraged her to take another step by tapping her with the end of the lead rope. Rewarding each try, and praising her a lot, developed Beauty's confidence. Before my time was up, Beauty was walking in and backing out of the trailer calmly.

I had no intention of saddling Beauty that third session, let alone sitting on her back. I had never gotten so far with a horse in such a short time. However, she was doing extremely well, and the saddle was there on the fence—it just seemed like the thing to do. I made sure Beauty was okay with each step before proceeding, and she accepted whatever I did with her. I was astonished when Michael, thanking me for the work I had done, said, "We thought for a long time that Beauty was an untrainable little mare."

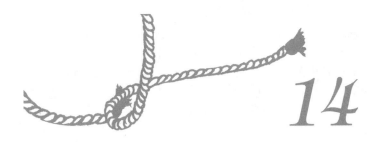

Rose's First Ride

M y plan was to have Kim do some ground work with Rose when I got in the saddle. That is a technique I have used successfully. It would give Rose a chance to do something familiar while getting used to carrying a rider. I didn't think Rose's entire world should change just because I got on her back. In fact, I had been doing ground work in a way intended to get Rose used to what she would feel when she was being ridden. Having a person on the ground working Rose the first time she felt the weight of a rider would make that transition even easier.

Emily, Rose's owner, had trailered her other horse over for a lesson with Kim. We had arranged it so I would be there to work with Rose after Emily's lesson. Kim and Emily watched while I prepared Rose to be ridden. Just as I was ready to get on, another of Kim's clients arrived for a lesson. Kim was not available to help me after all. I decided to just get on and ride. We had a good foundation of ground work. Rose was in a good place mentally. I knew she was ready.

When I got in the saddle, I sat there quietly, petting Rose for a minute or so. I always try not to move out right away when I get on. I don't want the horse to make a connection between getting on and going. Rose remained calm and seemed to be all right with me on her back. When I did ask Rose to move, the first few steps were tentative. She took a couple of steps backward, then sideways. I held the lead rope out to the side and slightly forward, trying to make the halter feel the same way it would if I were directing her out on a circle from the ground. Rose understood that feel and walked forward on a circle. I just blended in with her as she walked around the pen and stopped when she quit walking. When I was ready to go again, I directed her out on a circle the other way. Rose followed that direction so well that I decided to start seeing how much ground work I could duplicate from the saddle.

With a conscious effort to make my requests feel the same to Rose as they did when I was on the ground, I guided her through the repertoire of movements she was familiar with. Rose walked a circle and changed directions by disengaging her hind end, rocking back on her haunches, and stepping across with her shoulder. She moved from a small circle to a larger circle, stepping sideways and forward at the same time. She sidepassed along the fence. She tucked her head and backed. She backed quarter circles, right and left. Rose was doing all this with understanding. She was remaining calm and relaxed and was even yawning.

I rode for a few more minutes, demonstrating to Emily how Rose would follow my body when I focused my intention on a new place to go. Rose walked fast when I allowed the movement she was creating in me to get larger, and she walked slow when I slowed down my body. When I slowed that movement all the way to a stop, Rose stopped with me. I offered to let Emily ride her horse. She was surprised, not having expected to be riding that soon.

"As calm and controllable as she is," I told Emily, "the only danger is that Rose might fall asleep."

Emily had a great ride and repeated most of the maneuvers I had done. She was amazed at how well Rose followed her intention. I explained that the idea all along had been to develop that mental connection. The ground work was specifically intended to be a foundation of understanding that would carry over into the saddle. Most of the time you have enough working for you that you can be safe on that first ride and build on what's there. Rose's response was ideal; everything had carried over.

15

Trouble

I love working at Wendy's. It's hard to imagine a more
beautiful setting—pine trees flowing down from the rock
outcroppings that crown the ridge two thousand feet above.
The forest opens onto a beautiful meadow at her barn.
Fleetwood was feeling wonderful—light, responsive, following my focus, and steering effortlessly. He seemed to float
from a circle to a leg yield. He shouldered in as if he was
melting into my hands. I chuckled as I thought about the different feel of our first ride.

As I got in the saddle for that first ride, Fleetwood seemed
a little tense. I rubbed his neck and adjusted the reins as I settled in. Somehow the end of the rein flipped up and ticked
Fleetwood's ear. That was more than he could handle and he
took off like a shot. My first reaction, as we careened around
the round pen at what I thought was as fast as Fleetwood
could run, was to pick up a rein and try to bend him. That
upset Fleetwood even more and he ran faster. Next I attempt-
ed to reassure him by petting his neck. I figured some soothing strokes would calm Fleetwood down. Wrong! Fleetwood
found the movement behind his head very upsetting. He
generated even more speed. I took a good handhold of
mane, made sure I was balanced in the saddle, looked ahead
about a quarter of the way around the round pen, and began

taking very deep breaths in time with Fleetwood's stride. I accentuated the exhales, sinking down into the saddle with each breath.

I have no idea how many laps we made. Fleetwood seemed to run for a long time before he stopped near the gate. We were both out of breath. I was glad to have survived and decided to get off and do more ground work. When I moved my leg to take my right foot out of the stirrup, Fleetwood took off running again. On our third lap, I asked Wendy to come into the round pen. I thought she might be able to draw Fleetwood to her and get us stopped. I have used the technique of driving a horse around the round pen and backing off to hook them on quite often. I never gave much thought to how much trouble that driving might be for the horse, but from my position on Fleetwood's back, I could feel how much trouble it was for him. Every time Wendy moved, Fleetwood would tense up and run faster. I ended up asking Wendy to stand quietly in the center of the round pen without moving.

Fleetwood finally stopped and let me get off. I was left with a strong impression of how troublesome it was for him to be driven around the pen. That feeling has come back to me many times since. Now, when a horse I am trying to hook on gets lost and runs around the round pen, I find myself standing still and waiting for the horse, instead of driving harder in an attempt to make myself more meaningful. At my house, I have a blue plastic barrel to sit on. It is a very valuable accessory for my round pen.

16

Supporting Curl

M y stomach came up into my chest, and I got short of
breath as I saw the commotion below me. We were
descending a narrow set of switchbacks on a steep hillside.
Mary's horse had spooked and dropped a foot over the edge.
It was a tense moment, but they recovered nicely. I was glad
to be on the ground leading my horse.

I had gotten off Curl a couple of miles earlier on top of
the narrow ridge. Years of dude-string use had worn the trail
into a deep rut, and Curl was having a problem with that.
The ridge was narrow and I did not feel comfortable with the
way she kept jumping out of the rut, so I chose to walk. Now
we were coming off that ridge into the valley below.

When I reached the bottom, Grace commented on how
nice it was that I had a horse I could lead down a narrow trail
like that. She said her horse would crowd her too much and
she felt safer on its back. I pointed out that I had been working on having Curl stay back for the past two miles before we
got to the switchbacks. Even though I had been doing a lot of
walking on this trail ride, I was getting some good things
accomplished with my horse.

We were in an area none of us had ridden before, the
map we had was not detailed enough, and Curl was green.
We would have a good ride until the group became confused.

We would be riding along nicely and would come to a trail junction, and in the midst of the group's indecision, Curl would just fall apart. I didn't feel capable of handling the situation well in the saddle, so whenever that happened, I got off and walked. When the group was more focused, and Curl was in a good frame of mind, I got back on. I walked about eight miles that weekend, and Curl got exposed to a lot of varied terrain that I don't have around home. However, she was not overexposed from my lack of ability to handle the situation well from the saddle. I was concerned that I may be teaching Curl to act up whenever she wanted to get out of doing something; that proved not to be the case. It actually was a turning point in our relationship. After that experience, I was better able to support her when she was troubled, or should I say, she was better able to trust my support.

Here is my take on it. Horses know their survival depends on the herd leader. They are much more at ease following a leader; however, because of the way leadership is tied to their survival, they are ready to assume the leadership role. In other words, when I failed to be a worthy leader, Curl's self-preservation came into play, and she took over with ideas of her own. Much is involved in being a worthy leader. Having a clear plan in mind just happened to be the aspect of leadership to which Curl initially reacted. My insecurity in handling her in that situation quickly led to an avalanche of failure in other aspects of leadership. By getting off, I was able to put aside that insecurity and again be a worthy leader. There was no magic in getting off; it was simply what I needed to do to make the necessary change in my mental state. By giving Curl the experience of being able to trust me to be a worthy leader, our relationship strengthened. This is what I see as supporting the horse—being a worthy leader.

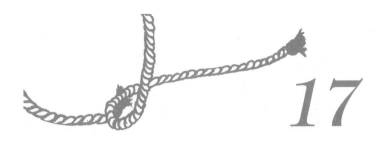

Loading Traveler

Polar Fleece® is sure nice stuff. I was thankful for the vest under my coat, the balaclava under my helmet, and my gloves. Cathy had almost canceled our appointment because of the weather, but she really wanted to head things off before her horse's problem became worse.

I watched as Cathy put Traveler into her new slant-load trailer. He didn't look totally comfortable to me. It looked like he could not move in the trailer, and if he needed to move, he had to get out. That, I believe, was the cause of the problem.

Cathy called me because Traveler had pulled back. She'd hauled him several times in her stock trailer without incident, but Cathy was not comfortable with that old trailer. In fact, it was preventing her from taking her horse places she wanted to go. Now that Traveler was being started under saddle, Cathy had upgraded to a nice, new gooseneck slant-load. The fact that Traveler was having a problem with such a nice trailer surprised her.

I began to work at getting Traveler comfortable with the new trailer. Sending him past me, I blocked his attempts to avoid the trailer and rewarded each move toward it with a release of pressure and petting. When Traveler reached the back end of the trailer, I tried to make that a comfortable

46

place, letting him investigate this new thing in his world. If he needed to leave, I didn't stop him but would send him right back to the trailer. At times, when he was calm and relaxed, I would take him to a spot I had picked and give him a break, petting him and keeping his attention on me. Working in this fashion, Traveler was soon walking into the trailer.

Next, I tried to get Traveler to move around in the trailer without getting out. At first, any time he moved his feet he would exit. I let him, and we would take a short break. This gave us lots of practice going in and out. Traveler was also learning that there were two places to be—with me where we took our breaks or in the trailer. As Traveler developed his ability to move around in the trailer, he also got better at going into it. I was having to do less and less to ask him to load up.

At this point, I replaced Traveler's halter with a sixty-foot lariat. I like to get a horse to load well enough so that I can send him into the trailer from a distance. Starting from the place we had been taking our breaks, I sent Traveler away from me and directed him just enough to keep his mind on the trailer. When it took less direction to keep him headed toward the trailer, I worked my way further and further away. I figured it was good when Traveler consistently walked into the trailer on his own from twenty feet away.

I now turned my attention to Cathy. I wanted to help her develop a routine for loading her horse. Besides, if she took over, it would give me a chance to take off some of the layers that were heating me up now that the sun had come out. We put Traveler's halter back on and Cathy stepped into the back of the trailer. As good as Traveler had just been loading, we were both surprised when he refused to lead past Cathy into the trailer.

Going back to what had just worked so well, I stood about five feet behind the trailer even with the left side. Putting the lead rope over Traveler's back, I sent him toward the trailer. Traveler walked right in and calmly positioned himself parallel to the slant wall. I stepped into the trailer and closed the divider; it was as if Traveler had done it like this all his life. When I opened the divider, Traveler remained calm and in place. I had to encourage him to come out by lifting his tail.

On my drive home, I thought about why Traveler did not want to load for Cathy. Then it struck me! In his eyes there wasn't enough room; he didn't want to crowd her on the way by. In my mind, loading from a distance was more difficult, but for Traveler, it was actually easier because I was not in his way.

Buck

Dale called to ask for some advice about his new horse. He had tried Buck out before purchasing him. They had ridden about an hour in an arena, then trailered to a trail where they had enjoyed a nice three-hour ride. Buck had performed beautifully in the arena and on the trail ride, but now that Dale had him home, Buck was a different animal. Not only was he nearly unmanageable, he was refusing to load in the trailer. After some discussion, I told Dale I thought he needed to alter his feeding program. It sounded to me like Buck was getting way more energy in his feed than he needed.

The next time Dale contacted me, he said the change he made in Buck's feed seemed to have an initial effect, but he still needed help. Over the next several weeks, Dale and I managed to get together a few times. We worked on getting Buck's attention in the round pen, developing our ability to communicate our intention through the lead rope, and we made some adjustments to improve the saddle's stability. It seemed to me like we were making progress with Buck, even if it was small steps, but there was no miraculous turn-around. Unfortunately, Dale's schedule was such that we couldn't maintain regular sessions, and I didn't hear from him for a while.

When Dale called again, he asked if I would take Buck in for two weeks while he was on vacation. He needed to have Buck taken care of while he was gone, and he thought he might as well be in training. Normally, I don't take a horse in for less than thirty days, but I knew Buck and Dale needed help, so I agreed. Dale brought Buck's feed with him and showed me how to mix his rations: two scoops of grain mix, a measuring cup of a hoof-care product, a couple of tablespoons of a digestive aid, and some other supplement. It all seemed a little much. Considering our earlier conversations about feeding programs, I wondered what Buck had been getting before.

Usually, it only takes a day or two for new horses arriving at our place to settle in. The third day after Buck arrived, he was still nervous and spooky. He seemed ultra-sensitive—wired, like he was on drugs. It didn't do a lot of good to try to train him in this condition, so I put him on our feeding program to see if that would calm him down. In the morning, Buck got only grass hay. At night, he got a small amount, about one-fourth of what Dale had been giving him, of a lower-protein grain mix and a vitamin/mineral supplement in addition to his hay. In two feedings, Buck made a major personality change. In two days, he was a different horse. To verify that it was the feed, and not that it just took Buck that long to get comfortable with his new surroundings, I put him back on his old feeding program. Two days later Buck was that wired, spooky horse again. I switched back to my feed, and Buck returned to a calm, natural state. The day Dale came to pick up his horse, he had what he described as "The best ride I've ever had on Buck."

19

Patterns and Feel

I was puzzled as I watched Lynn working her horse in the hay field. I liked how soft and responsive Rose seemed. She went out on a circle with very gentle direction and no additional support. She stepped her hind foot under nicely, rocked back and came across with the shoulder; it all looked good. I'd been trying to help Lynn figure out why some days she had an extraordinarily good time, and other days she was barely able to keep Rose under control. I knew this inconsistency should show up in the ground work. Then it hit me. As good as it looked physically, there was no mental connection between Rose and Lynn. I asked Lynn if she would like to see a different way to put her ground work exercises together, just to break up the monotony. She agreed, offering me the lead rope.

Leaving the shade of the cottonwood tree, I walked out into the grass, still damp from the last irrigation. I asked Rose to move her shoulder one step. She went out on a circle. I stopped her and tried again with the same result. Bending Rose toward me, I asked for her hip to yield away one step. Rose walked her hind end around her front end for half a circle and lined up facing me. Although Rose was moving calmly and responding to soft suggestions, the feel I presented was not communicating my intent; it was cueing a pattern. That's where the mental connection had broken down.

This is exactly what Bill Dorrance talks about in his book, *True Horsemanship Through Feel*. He says, "Don't get into a pattern and repeat the same thing over and over again because the horse will stay more responsive to your feel if there's variety worked into the things you do with him. The main problem with patterns is that the horse gets so he can't follow a feel outside that pattern. You don't want the horse to get an idea that he should be making any moves towards something he thinks is correct if it means that he avoids your feel to do it, because that's the horse taking over—and he's liable to do that if he's just rehearsing those patterns."

A hawk landed in one of the trees at the edge of the field and seemed to watch me as I worked with Rose one step at a time. I prepared her, getting the right bend in her body and shifting her balance to unweight the foot I wanted her to move. Then I did as little as possible to move that foot, releasing as soon as the movement started. If Rose did more than I asked, I stopped her and put her feet back where I wanted them. This level of precision resulted in getting her mind focused on me—on understanding and acting on my intent.

Several months later, while Lynn and I were riding on the mesa behind the ranch, I commented how great it was to have a calm, steady horse like Rose to support my youngster. I was impressed with the adjustment Lynn had made. Breaking out of her own pattern, she and Rose had regained their mental connection. Now Rose was the calm, consistent horse Lynn had been striving for.

20

A Round Pen Experiment

I'd been trying to reduce the amount of dust that flies when I work with horses. About the time I began to think the only way to keep the dust down was to water the round pen, I tried a little experiment with three horses I had in training.

First I sent Magic around the pen, doing as little as possible to keep her moving faster than a walk. With my shoulders squared up, I looked her straight in the eye. My intention was to keep at this until she lowered her head, indicating she was ready to join up. Occasionally, Magic would lick her lips, but she never lowered her head. When I felt she had run around enough, I backed off and allowed her to stop. Magic stopped parallel to the fence, stiff, with her head high. I turned her and we went the other way. The results were the same—Magic never lowered her head. I decided that was enough and put her up.

My plan with Red was to watch for the slightest indication he was ready to hook on. At the flick of an ear, or the tip of the nose, I would back off to draw him in. The first half dozen times I backed off, Red continued around the pen. When I cut him off, he would slide to a stop and change directions, sending up a cloud of dust. It took some time before Red would stop and face me. Then, continuing in this manner for several more minutes, he got to where he would walk up to me. By the time we achieved that success, we were both tired and sweaty.

I knew Blaze would be difficult. The last time I turned him loose in the round pen I'd been unable to catch him. I took off his halter and sat on a plastic barrel, purposely doing nothing to influence his actions. I watched the moon peeking in and out of the clouds. I enjoyed the cool evening breeze, so refreshing after a hot day. Kim sat in a chair outside the pen, and we discussed the difficult trailer loading she had just done. Before long, Blaze was standing in front of me, allowing me to rub his forehead. I got off the barrel, and he followed me as I walked some circles and figure-eights.

It fascinated me that doing nothing yielded better results than either of the other techniques. I was impressed with the idea that it is far better to fit the horse than to mimic a particular method. I felt I had lived Bill Dorrance's words, "If he's not bothered about you being nearby, or about any other thing, then it's just going to be a matter of time before his curiosity and his intelligence get to working on the idea that you might be there for a useful purpose that he has in mind."

Working Curl at Liberty

We had quit riding Curl a month before her foal was due; her job for the summer had been to raise Prairie. Now, late in the fall, we were anxious to restart her. It had been cold and windy for several days, but a break in the weather gave Kim a chance to get Curl out.

Curl hadn't been touchy about her flanks with the foal; we had worked for months to desensitize her. Now, however, she was hunkering down when touched there. Thinking she would have to start all over, Kim removed her glove. With smooth, long strokes, she moved her hand closer to Curl's flank. Kim continued until she could reach under Curl's hind legs and massage the gunk out from between her teats. Curl started to work her mouth, the way she would if she were grooming another horse. The deeper Kim rubbed, the more Curl worked her mouth.

When she finished cleaning between Curl's teats, Kim picked up a curry comb. Starting along Curl's neck, and working her way back, Kim noticed a big change when she reached Curl's stomach and flank. There was no tightness in the leg or in the croup, and Curl wasn't sinking down! She wasn't back at square one; what we had established before Prairie was born was still there.

Happy not to be starting from scratch, Kim took Curl to the round pen. As soon as Curl was loose, she started to snuffle around for grass. Kim meandered to the middle of the ring, preparing to drive Curl off to get her attention. As Kim turned around, she had to immediately change her thought, because Curl was walking toward her. She already had her attention.

Kim moved Curl off to check out her transitions. Curl went from a walk to a flat-foot walk and then into a very rhythmic fox trot. Kim wanted to see her canter. Before the foal was born, we had been working on cantering without cross-firing. Curl moved up very freely into the canter and was right on—no cross-fire.

Curl began to play with our dog, Shelby, who was running around the outside of the round pen. Curl galloped, cantered, twisted, and bucked with the freest movements I've ever seen from her. Kim backed up, asking Curl to hook on and come to her. Curl responded with ease. After a pet, Kim sent Curl out again, this time to see how she was at changing eyes. Curl turned when Kim put the lead rope in her other hand.

Sensing Curl's responsiveness, Kim moved to the side of the round pen opposite Curl. From that distance, she was able to direct Curl in a figure-eight, stop her, and hook her on. What a kick! Curl stayed hooked on so well, Kim asked her to move her hind end by looking and pointing a finger at her. Then Kim moved Curl's front feet by looking and pointing at her shoulder. Then, out of curiosity, Kim asked Curl to move both ends by pointing with both fingers. Curl did a great side pass. She did it again, so we knew it wasn't a coincidence. Curl side passed a third time! Kim was elated and quit on that note.

It's hard to explain why that day with Curl meant so much. Ray Hunt talks about a kinship with the horse—when it feels good to you, and it feels good to the horse. Well, it felt good that day. It wasn't expected, and Kim wasn't trying to achieve it. It was the result of a series of situations Kim had set up and let happen. She just worked with what presented itself. The best part was, Curl exceeded our expectations after an eight-month layoff. Horses do remember what we teach them.

The Effect of Thought

P egus was troubled when I started working with her. She had made great progress and was getting nice. One particular day she was melting into my hands and coming through very soft. I'd work on something a little bit, she would really come through, and then things would just fall apart. I'd get her busy, she'd get nice, and about the time she really came through, things fell apart again. When that happened enough times for me to realize it was not a coincidence, I started looking for the cause. I paid close attention as I asked her for a specific maneuver. She did well but not great. I rewarded the effort, then asked again, making sure I was riding as precisely as possible. She melted—her movement was so balanced and fluid and her body so soft. "That was perfect," I thought to myself. "I sure don't need to practice that anymore. What shall I work on next?" In that moment of indecision, Pegus fell apart.

I was starting Chief for Mary. When Chief was born, he was the surviving foal from a pair of twins. It took a lot to keep him alive, and that initial handling seemed to create a chip on his shoulder. Chief's attitude had Mary intimidated—for good reason—but he was making some nice changes now. I was trying to show Mary how well Chief was responding by having her work him in the round pen. After some initial hooking on and ground work, we had saddled Chief, and

Mary was moving him out. When Chief went into a canter, he started bucking—something he had not done for me in quite some time. "See that!" Mary exclaimed. "I knew he was going to buck. I could feel it from the time I came in here."

A young riding student once helped me experiment with the effect the rider's thoughts have on the horse. I asked Ann to think about something that made her nervous and anxious. When she got that thought fixed in her mind, I had her ride out on the rail. Ann was attempting to go to the right, but Chip would have nothing of it. He acted as if death awaited him in that direction. Chip is a well-trained school horse, but no matter how much Ann bent him, he was pushing through her and going the other way. After they went about thirty feet, I had Ann stop. This time I asked her to think about something she liked—something relaxing and comforting. When Ann had that thought fixed in her mind, I asked her to ride out. Chip went calmly with her, in the direction he had just refused to go. As she rode down the rail, thinking that nice thought, I asked Ann to picture the horse walking in a circle, without actually cueing him to turn. Chip made the nicest turn you could imagine.

23

The Head Shy Horse Who Wasn't Head Shy

M argaret had been watching me work with her friend Cindy's horse. She was interested in what I was doing because she was having some problems with her own horse, Banner. The problem was Margaret was on a limited budget and couldn't afford regular training sessions. I hesitated, trying to think of the best way to answer her, when she asked if I could cure a horse of head shyness in one session. Finally, I told her that, if Banner was truly head shy, I probably couldn't, but I could show her how I would work on it and maybe she could take it from there. We made an appointment for the next week, and I left with an uneasy feeling, thinking of several cases of head shyness I had dealt with that were serious, long-term projects.

When I arrived at the farm where Margaret boarded Banner, they were enjoying the shade of the trees in the backyard. It was a nice place for the farrier to trim the horse's feet. As I watched Margaret holding Banner, it was the picture of understanding and contentment. I didn't see any indication that the horse was unsure or defensive about anything. When I mentioned how nice he was acting, Margaret said Banner was really good about everything until you touched his ears. When the farrier was done, we found an open place in front of the barn where we would have some room to work.

Margaret explained that Banner had started throwing his head up when she tried to bridle him. Thinking she should not do anything that bothered her horse, Margaret backed off every time Banner's head went up and petted him to calm him down. Someone had advised her to unbuckle the cheek piece of the headstall and put it on like a halter. This way she wouldn't have to slide the bridle over her horse's ears. That had worked for a while, but now Banner reacted every time her hands got near his ears and she was not able to bridle him at all. This was very frustrating because he was so good once the bridle was on. However, not being able to bridle Banner was keeping her from riding him.

I took the lead rope from Margaret and reached up to touch Banner's ears. His head popped up so quickly his front feet came off the ground. When his feet came back down, he backed up a few steps with his head still up in the air, then stopped and relaxed. It was an impressive display, and I could see how it would be intimidating, but I saw no panic and no attempt to escape. It looked to me like Banner had been taught to do a trick. To test that idea, I prepared to touch his ear again. This time I was ready for his reaction. I held the cheek piece of the halter with one hand so I could stay with him and lightly grasped his ear with my other hand. I went with Banner's motion as his head went up, and he took a few steps back. When he stopped, I let go of his ear, and he was as relaxed as if nothing had happened.

I explained to Margaret that by getting released every time he threw his head up, Banner had learned he was supposed to do that whenever someone touched his ear. I continued rubbing Banner's ear and grasping it lightly with my cupped hand. I would follow Banner's motion and release after his feet stopped, when his head started to come down. It didn't take long for Banner to quit moving his feet. Soon he wasn't raising his head at all. The conditioned response had been disassociated from the cue.

Because Banner had learned to display such a dramatic

action, I decided to teach him to do something else when his ear was touched. With a light pressure from my hand on his ear, I offered Banner a feel to lower his head and bring it to me. I released his ear every time he started to lower his head. It wasn't long before Banner would lower his head and bring it around to the position it needed to be in for bridling. Just by changing what Banner got released for, we changed a response that kept Margaret from bridling him to a response that would help her. Margaret now had a cue to get Banner to put his head in position to be bridled. All she needed to do was touch his ear.

We spent the rest of the session having Margaret practice getting Banner in position to bridle, putting the bridle on, and taking it off. To Margaret, this change in her horse seemed like a miracle. I told her that Banner was never head shy. He was just a very bright horse that had inadvertently been taught a conditioned response to the cue of touching his ear. I had simply taught him a different response to that cue. We all need to be careful about what we are teaching our horses through our releases. The difference between a stupid horse that is so head shy you can't bridle him, and an intelligent horse that learns cues very quickly, may lie in being aware of what we are releasing for.

Curl and the Grand Canyon

C url had become Kim's main riding horse during the last several months. Kim really wanted to build Curl's confidence. We had been selecting trails with care over the past months because Curl is a spooky mare. We started by trailering her to different arenas. Then we rode her on easy trails, like abandoned jeep roads, and finally graduated to narrower trails.

This was Curl's third or fourth mountain trail ride. Kim really liked the way Curl was moving. Her movements were free, she was fox trotting with energy and rhythm, and her flat-foot walk was exceptionally smooth. Kim had been riding in the middle of the pack or at the tail end of our small group. Curl seemed brave, so Kim let her take a short turn in the lead. Places we thought Curl might have trouble leading the group, like through thickets of brush and shadowed areas, were no problem.

The trail-maintenance crews had done a splendid job on trail maintenance. They had built several new water bars and bridges and raised the trails through boggy areas. At one point, the trail meandered in an S-curve through some springs to a bridge. This area had been lined with large timbers, then filled with dirt and pink rock. Culverts and ditches drained water away from this raised portion of the trail. Just before the step up onto the bridge, there was a large thicket. A sawhorse, poised at the edge of the brush as if ready to pounce, was partially blocking the trail. The brush, which was moving in the breeze, cast long shadows across the pink rock and the bridge.

Curl immediately put on the brakes, ready to turn tail and run. Kim blocked the escape and reassured Curl with a soft voice. Petting Curl to calm her down, Kim used long strokes and scratching along Curl's mane—something she really likes.

They stood there for a few minutes. Kim tried to look at the trail from Curl's point of view. She thought this scene must be like looking out over the Grand Canyon with only a narrow rope bridge to go across—initially a frightening image—then, as if in a movie studio, you realize the canyon is a painting and the bridge is only raised an inch off the floor.

As they stood there together, Curl must have come to the same realization. She appeared to scope the area out and think out a game plan. Then she started to walk toward the bridge. Curl did give some concerned looks and a few snorts at the dark ditches—like spider legs—coming out from under the raised trail as she maneuvered along the pink rock, stepped around the sawhorse and up onto the bridge, and walked to the other side. Curl looked like she was very proud of herself. I was proud of her, too.

This incident made me understand more about waiting on the horse. Curl wanted to try. Had Kim pushed the issue, she would have discouraged Curl's future tries. But waiting on Curl, letting her think things through, encouraged Curl to try more.

25

Driving Through Mud

May's horse, Flash, sure had me thinking about getting with a horse's feel and getting together with the horse mentally. On page 143 of his book, *True Horsemanship Through Feel*, Bill Dorrance says, "The person has got to flow with that horse's movements and understand the intentions in that horse's mental system, the best way he can, in order to get this better connection through feel working both ways." Flash had developed a vast repertoire of evasions. Every time I asked her for something, she would do something different. We seemed so far from the connection Bill Dorrance described.

I had helped May start Flash by coaching her once a week. May did a great job, but Flash had reached a point where she was taking over with ideas of her own. For several weeks I had been riding Flash during our lessons. When things felt good, May would get on and do what I had just done. In this way, May was able to feel what it should be like. During the week, May would ride Flash, making note of the problems she was having. I would work on those problems in our next lesson. On this particular day, we decided to work in the hay field. May felt they were doing well in the arena, but she was having trouble controlling Flash out in the open.

I focused on a tree in the distance and started to ride Flash across the field. She had a different plan in mind. Instead of trying to overpower the evasion, I blended in with her, adjusting my body as if I had asked for that move. It felt soft in a stride or two, so I directed Flash back on course for the tree. It wasn't long before she tried something else. Again, I adjusted so that I was asking her to do what she had tried on her own. When it felt like we were together again, I directed her back on course. And so it went across the field a few strides at a time.

Getting with Flash's feel—that is, blending with her rhythm, with the placement of her feet, with her balance, and with her energy level—created a comfortable equilibrium for her. This allowed her to recognize when I offered the feel for a change. When she felt me change, she adjusted to maintain the equilibrium. When I felt Flash begin to respond, I blended in. This blending was more than just a release to tell her she did what I wanted. It was a matching of balance and rhythmic energy so that we could go together again in comfortable equilibrium. This was the point where my idea and Flash's idea became the same idea at the same time.

Working at it this way kept Flash from getting upset, and we had lots of opportunities to experience that feeling of being together. We did make it to our destination, although it felt like driving in slippery mud.

26

Suppling Boe

B oe is one of those cases I wish I had videotaped, because his "before and after" were so dramatic. He really demonstrated the importance of shape and suppleness and showed me they were related to more than just physical development. Claire asked me to take a look at him because he had started balking on the trail. He would just stop and refuse to go. The only way Claire was able to get him to continue was to ride him in a circle; once she had some momentum, she could direct him out the way she wanted to go.

I have been working for some time with the idea of an ideal frame within which a horse should work. This ideal frame is balanced, supple, and structurally strong. I start developing it on the ground, but it continues in the saddle. I look for specific muscles to be engaged and other muscles to be relaxed. To get the proper effect, the horse must give you that frame. If you make it happen, you can get the horse's body in the same shape, but the muscle usage will be different. This is because muscles you don't want engaged will be engaged in resisting the pressure you are using to cause that shape.

Boe had been ridden for ten years with no regard to the way he was using his body. Although he is about the most "bomb-proof" horse I've ever seen, I did a couple of ground-work sessions with Boe before I rode him. He was stiff and resistant—a long way from the ideal frame I had in mind. After the first session, I noticed that he had started to use his head as he walked back to the barn. When he had come out, his head had looked like it was a block glued onto a board. As he walked back, his head nodded with each step; there was a definite hinge between his head and neck.

During the next few sessions, I worked on getting Boe to bend through his rib cage and step under with his hind leg. This was a real problem for him because he tended to push off with that inside hind leg instead of stepping under and lifting with it. This was real evident when I rode him. I've never had so much trouble staying balanced on a horse in my life. Every time he turned, I got thrown to the outside. Beyond the physical aspect of this way Boe was using his body, I had a most unusual sensation. It was the first time in a very long time that I felt like a separate entity sitting on top of a horse trying to tell him what to do. Boe was so broke, I got on him sooner than I would have if he had been a troubled horse. I normally get a horse a lot better at doing ground work, and through that, I establish a mental connection—an understanding of my intention—before I get in the saddle.

During the next couple of sessions, the wind was blowing so strongly I just did ground work with Boe. One week, Claire and I took Boe and a younger horse we were working with on a walk up the leeward side of the mountain. It was not as windy there as it was in the open valley. We used the walk to work on getting the horses to follow our speed—keeping track of us to know how fast to go. The next week, Claire sat in her truck and watched me work in the round pen. The wind was blowing hard enough to rock Claire's truck and snow was blowing off the roof of the barn, onto Boe and me.

During that session, Boe really came through. As his understanding increased, he started giving me the frame I was looking for. He would bend and stay balanced in the turns.

He quit pushing off with that inside hind foot and started reaching under himself and lifting with it. He rocked back and supported his weight on his haunches when he stepped across with his shoulder. He even gave me a great soft feel and rounded his back when he backed up. I was so glad I hadn't wimped out and not worked with him because of the weather.

The next time I rode Boe, he was a different horse. It felt like he was right with me, following my intention and staying so soft and balanced in his turns. His stride had lengthened and become more evenly cadenced, making his gait much smoother. Claire said seeing him work like that was the perfect Christmas present. He no longer moved like a mechanical wind-up toy.

Letting Curl Cross
the Creek

There is an interesting balance between blending in with a horse and letting the horse take over with its own ideas. In his book, *True Horsemanship Through Feel*, Bill Dorrance says, "Until the horse is ready to look to you for the direction and support he needs so he can stay relaxed and follow your feel, you need to follow his feel." That doesn't mean you should just let the horse take over with its own ideas every time he shows a little resistance to what you ask. There are, however, situations where you can get in the way of the horse's best work if you insist on being in control. Curl demonstrated this at one of our trail-ride clinics.

We still considered Curl to be pretty green. While she was beginning to come into herself, she lacked the experience of a seasoned trail horse. This was the first ride in which Curl was given the responsibility of leading the group. It was fascinating to watch her negotiate difficult obstacles without another horse going first. Kim was doing a great job of reassuring and supporting Curl.

Everyone on the ride was enjoying the beautiful, sunny, spring day as we rode up the valley between Horsetooth Mountain's steep, wooded hillside and the red rimrock surrounding Horsetooth Reservoir. We crossed several wooden footbridges and passed a couple of coves where there were breaks in the cliffs. The trail occasionally went through patches of thick brush. Based on the horses' reaction, these must have been harboring some form of wildlife. Cresting the rise we had been riding toward, we saw the cross-country jump course open out in front of us.

We spent some time meandering through the cross-country course. Riding past the jumps was interesting. Made to look like rock walls, wagons, low sheds, and old corrals, they provided great distraction for the horses. I was impressed with how well Kim was getting Curl past these obstacles. Visualizing Curl walking calmly by the jump, Kim used the strong focus of hard eyes to guide Curl on the path she wanted to take. When they actually walked past the obstacle, Kim rewarded Curl with the relaxation of changing her focus to soft eyes. Using this technique, the encouragement of Kim's reins and legs was enough to support Curl through the course of scary obstacles without a spooking incident.

As we left the jump course, the trail took us through an icy water crossing at the bottom of a steep, narrow gully filled with lots of big rocks and bushes. Curl stopped at the edge of the water. Kim didn't treat this as a refusal by demanding that Curl keep going; rather, she stopped with Curl and let Curl look things over. Curl didn't act spooky or try to turn around—she just studied the situation for a minute and walked across. As Curl started to cross, Kim went with her, letting Curl pick her own way. I have never seen a horse place its feet more carefully or precisely than Curl did crossing that creek. I'm positive it would not have looked as pretty if Kim had insisted on being "in control." There are some times when the horse is the more capable partner.

Horses Helping Kids

Kim and I partner with a local alternative high school in a class called Reading, Writing, and Riding. The program incorporates two hours a week in the classroom and two hours a week at our place. In the classroom, students read articles about horse training and books on the general subject of horses. They write reports and essays about what they read, and they keep a journal. At our place, they work for us for one hour and get a riding lesson. Projects they work on include painting our fence, stacking hay, and cleaning pens. The program is funded mostly by a grant, but the kids have to pay a nominal fee each week. Including the chores and the nominal payment was a way to give the kids responsibility for being able to experience the horses. This creates a respect that I don't believe would be there if they were just given the opportunity.

It is touching to see the change that interacting with horses creates in these kids. One young girl, Joanne—the mother of a two-year-old son—went from a fearful, "I can't do this" attitude to a confident, "this is fun" attitude. Her teacher said she had become more confident in other areas of her life as well because of her interaction with our horses. Then there was Irene. She had been put into a foster home because of an altercation that put her mother in the hospital. Irene always seemed troubled and withdrawn. One week, I saw her soften and really enjoy her ride on Chip. When I mentioned it, Irene's teacher told me how much Irene looked forward to her riding lessons. They were the only positive aspect of her life.

Our school horses seem to know when these special students need extra care. On one occasion, Chip was paired with a student who had been in a coma—the result of injuries suffered in a bad car accident. Janet had mobility challenges and trouble with her speech. Two of the school's staff members assisted Janet, one on each side of her, as she groomed Chip and led him around. At first, Chip seemed to think he was with the staffer nearest to him, but when he made the connection to Janet, he shifted gears.

Chip softened noticeably. When they walked, he turned his head to look right at Janet and waited for her to come along. At one point, Janet's helper became anxious, thinking Chip was crowding Janet too much. Chip had actually moved into Janet to balance her when she became unstable. Once Janet recovered, Chip stepped away. Through interacting with Chip—grooming, leading, and doing simple ground work—Janet's balance, speech, and ability to walk improved noticeably.

Our class is not a therapy program. The intention is to use interaction with horses to motivate the students to read and write. The fact that the horses have such an impact on the kids makes it very rewarding. To see the horses put so much effort into meeting the kid's needs is thrilling.

Loading Moon Dust

M oon Dust had made a nice change in the six weeks he spent with me. Francis was thrilled. Having just had a wonderful ride, she was anticipating taking Moon Dust home the following weekend. As Francis and I relaxed in the warm afternoon sun for a few minutes, she told me how difficult Moon Dust was to load in her trailer. After having him pull away from her and run off into the woods, she came up with a system that seemed to be working for her, but she really wanted it improved.

Francis would lead Moon Dust to the back of her trailer and clip him to a lead rope she had tied there. Moon Dust would pull back and fight with the lead rope for a while before settling down. When Moon Dust quit fighting, Francis would switch lead ropes, clipping him to a lead rope she had tied inside the trailer. Moon Dust would pull and fight again for a little while before walking into the trailer. As Francis described this technique to me she said Moon Dust just needed to know there was no way out of it before he would decide to get in the trailer. I told Francis I would make a project out of getting Moon Dust to load better and assured her that he would be fine when she took him home.

I started my project by loading Moon Dust into my big stock trailer because it is less confining than Francis's small two-horse trailer. With the trailer positioned to give me a large, clear working area, I led Moon Dust up to the door. He turned and walked away rather briskly. I didn't get the feeling that he was trying to escape; rather, it seemed that was what he thought he was supposed to do. When I had the angle on Moon Dust, I set myself, and he hit the end of the lead rope. Moon Dust turned and faced me. He seemed a little surprised but not scared. I took him back to the trailer, petted him as he stood there, and took him away before he felt he needed to leave on his own. I then began a pattern of approach and retreat. Sending Moon Dust away from me, I would do as little directing as possible—just enough to keep him headed toward the trailer. When he got as far as he could go that time, I would take Moon Dust away and start again. By petting and praising him when he was interested in the trailer, Moon Dust was soon making an effort to get in—first his head, then his head and neck, then a front foot, then both front feet, then a back foot—until he was walking all the way in. After Moon Dust walked calmly into the trailer several times, I put him up.

Several days after loading Moon Dust into my stock trailer, I had a free afternoon so I could take the time to work with loading Moon Dust into Francis's trailer. I parked the trailer near the round pen, where I would have plenty of room to work. When I led Moon Dust toward the trailer, he stopped about fifteen feet away—frozen, planted, with his front feet spread apart, leaning back on his haunches and his attention riveted on the trailer. I petted Moon Dust and spoke to him in soothing tones, assuring him that everything was all right. It took a minute or two, but soon Moon Dust relaxed. I made sure he was with me by asking him to lower his head and by placing his feet back and forth. Then we proceeded to the trailer. Moon Dust never made an effort to leave. By using the same approach-and-retreat pattern I had used with the stock trailer, Moon Dust was soon walking into Francis's trailer calmly. When Moon Dust had gone in and out of the trailer several times and was staying in it until I asked him to come out, I decided to take it up a notch and see if he could learn to go in completely on his own.

Replacing Moon Dust's halter with a sixty-foot lariat, I picked a spot about twenty-five feet away from the trailer. I wanted Moon Dust to learn that there were two places to be—with me at that spot, or in the trailer. When I sent Moon Dust away, I let the rope feed out of my hand and only directed him when he lost interest in the trailer. We began a series of "be with me at our spot, now go get in the trailer." At first I had to walk along with him, back near his hip. As things progressed, I could be further and further away until I could stay at our spot and Moon Dust would walk into the trailer with very little directing. The last time I sent Moon Dust away, he started to go toward the horse that was in the round pen instead of the trailer. Before I managed to pick up the slack in my rope to direct Moon Dust back, he turned in the direction of the trailer. I was taking up rope as Moon Dust's path created slack now and didn't notice soon enough that he wasn't headed for the trailer—he was headed for the grassy ditch bank under the cottonwood tree. Just before I moved to drive Moon Dust away from the ditch, he stopped, looked at the trailer, turned, walked over, and got in. I called that good enough.

When Francis was ready to take Moon Dust home, she asked me to show her my procedure for loading. I led Moon Dust to Francis's trailer, opened the back door, put the lead rope over Moon Dust's back, asked him to get in, and stepped back out of his way. Moon Dust walked right in and stood there while I hooked the butt chain and closed the door.

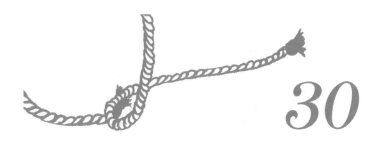

Curl, the Chicken, and Leadership

A s I talked to Angela about the lesson we had just finished, I found she was just as uncomfortable riding in an arena as I was. We both had felt crowded and had tried to get our horses away from the other horses in the arena. I had felt that no matter what I did, the others were drawn to me. Angela said she had tried to find an open spot, too, but no matter what she did, she couldn't get her horse away from mine. I thought back to when I first felt the other horses being drawn to me and tried to remember what had happened just prior to that.

I was riding Curl since Prince had injured his leg the day before. When I started Curl, I had put her in situations for which she was not prepared. As a result, she had scared me several times. It got to the point that my fear was keeping her from making much progress. At that point, Kim took over Curl's training. I had only ridden Curl a couple of times in the year before this lesson, and it had taken me a while to get relaxed on her; I still thought of her as the horse I was afraid of.

We were riding in an indoor arena on a hot summer day. The overhead door, midway down the long side, was open about two feet for ventilation. As I approached the door, a chicken ran into the arena. I felt Curl's body bend as she quickly looked at the chicken, poised for her escape. I focused straight down the wall of the arena to the corner as if my life depended on getting there. Curl's body straightened, and she walked a straight line past the door. The chicken ran back out the door to keep from getting trampled.

Noticing the effect my increased focus had on Curl, I began to do more than just look where we were going; I looked with a meaningful intent. I picked out a specific place to ride to, like the knot hole in that board, and Curl seemed to go there with a purpose. That's when things started to get crowded.

I rode deep into the corners, I cut across the arena, I circled to get behind the other horses; but they seemed to be drawn to me. It gave me an eerie feeling. I became conscious of the flow of my intent through my horse drawing the other horses along. They had recognized a leader and were choosing to follow.

When I told Angela how that had felt, she said, "I know! No matter what I did, my horse would follow yours. I even tried to circle and go the other way, but I couldn't get him to go anywhere Curl wasn't."

31

The Gift of a Ride

I was really enjoying this ride! The trail following Middle St. Vrain Creek into the Indian Peaks Wilderness Area was beautiful. I loved the aroma of the pines, the sound of the rushing brook cascading down the rocks, and the freshness of the cool mountain air. But it was how well my horse, Prince, and I were communicating that was making this ride so special. Months of effort had blossomed into a thrilling unity.

For the most part, I let Prince decide how to negotiate the rocky trail; but there were spots where I would make that decision, and I'd guide him with a light neck rein. When Prince looked off into the woods, concerned about a sound or smell, I reassured him by rubbing the reins lightly against his neck. If he got interested in grass alongside the trail, lifting the reins slightly repositioned his head. I marveled at the subtlety of our communication and reminisced about how it got to be this way.

First, I quit pulling Prince around with the reins. Instead, I used the reins to help shape and balance him. It was my responsibility to prepare him for the step I wanted. When I did this, the reins became a lot more meaningful.

Next, I began to steer by focusing on where I wanted to go, directing Prince's attention to that place and allowing his natural curiosity to take him there. This opened the door to a whole new level of lightness. I found it didn't take much to direct his attention—perhaps a slight lifting of the rein, the rolling of a toe, or even just shifting my body. With this approach, I became much more in tune with Prince mentally.

Being more aware of Prince's attention enabled me to anticipate his apprehension. By noticing sooner, it took less to support him, and he gave me a higher level of trust. It was as if Prince decided I wasn't out to lunch after all. I was there for him when he needed me, and all it took to reassure him was my rubbing him lightly on the neck with the reins.

The last step toward lightness involved blending in with Prince's movements. I needed to do more than just stay loose—I needed to feel the movement. Feeling that movement and going with it eliminated the brace Prince used to protect himself from my jolting in the saddle. That made it easier for him to negotiate the rough terrain.

Eating my lunch in a grassy meadow by the creek, I felt so small. I was awed by the magnificence of the cliffs towering above me and humbled by the gift Prince had given me.